A concisely written, pastorally focused, gospel-infused account of the place of suffering in the Christian life. A perfect guide to aid troubled souls find peace and comfort when the storm breaks.

DEREK W. H. THOMAS,
Senior Minister, First Presbyterian Church,
Columbia, South Carolina,
The Robert Strong Professor of Systematic and Historical Theology,
Reformed Theological Seminary, Atlanta, Georgia

Here is one small book addressing one monumental subject in the one essential way—filling our minds with and directing our hearts to the truths of Scripture. Brian Cosby serves the church and those suffering well with this helpful, pastoral, and wise volume on suffering. In these pages you will find help with a reality we all must wrestle with and will eventually experience to some degree.

JASON HELOPOULOS,
Associate Pastor, University Reformed Church,
East Lansing, Michigan and author of
A Neglected Grace: Family Worship in the Christian Home

If you find yourself wandering in the valley of the shadow of death and see no signs to show you the way through, pick up this little book and read it! It offers sound, Christ-centered, biblical, and yet eminently practical counsel on suffering.

J. V. FESKO,
Academic Dean, Professor of Systematic and Historical Theology,
Westminster Seminary California, Escondido, California

A CHRISTIAN'S POCKET GUIDE TO

SUFFERING

HOW GOD SHAPES US THROUGH PAIN AND TRAGEDY

BRIAN H. COSBY

paperback ISBN 978-1-78191-646-9
epub ISBN 978-1-78191-696-4
mobi ISBN 978-1-78191-697-1

10 9 8 7 6 5 4 3 2 1

Published in 2015
by
Christian Focus Publications Ltd,
Geanies House, Fearn, Ross-shire,
IV20 1TW, Scotland, Great Britain

www.christianfocus.com

Cover design by Daniel Van Straaten

Printed by Nørhaven, Denmark

CONTENTS

To
Betsy Harris
one of the most joyful and courageous sufferers
I've known

⚠ Warning
🖉 Don't Forget
⑦ Stop and Think
❋ Point of Interest

PREFACE

When tragedy strikes—the death of a child, hurricanes, a school shooting—we begin looking for an escape from the pain, a way out, or we clamor for answers from a panel of religious 'experts' to explain the ever-present question, 'Why?' We want answers and we want to believe that our suffering is not meaningless.

Unfortunately, our culture strives to deny the reality of death and suffering and we in the West continually long to drink from the fountain of youth—expressed in our endless pursuit of Botox treatments, anti-aging cream, cosmetic surgeries, and hair dyes. We cloak funerals as 'celebrations' and convey the empty promise that all people go to heaven (except perhaps Hitler and Stalin). We cannot handle the harsh reality of suffering and so we hide behind the virtual walls of social media where we pretend our venerable hearts are safe from rejection, grief, and the evil 'out there.' Yet, all the while, you and I know it is there, it is real, and it is painful.

Maybe you have picked up this book because you are in the throes of affliction or because you are trying to minister to someone who is. I want to be honest from the outset: this book will not give you empty clichés for a feel-good faith or half-truths that mask the pain. No, this book seeks to simply but clearly present a biblical view of suffering so that your feet might land on the solid foundation of God's Word and the God of that Word and, *there*, find understanding and hope. All other ground is sinking sand.

1

WHERE DOES SUFFERING COME FROM?

Suffering has a way of leading us to ask the really fundamental and difficult questions. In an instant, it can peel back the external layers of performing and pretense—leaving us begging for mercy, for relief, for escape, and for hope. Something about suffering does not seem natural and, yet, we see and experience its devastating reality everyday on the news, across the nation, and in our families.

Most of the time, the question we ask (or assume to answer) is, 'Why?' We long to find some sense of meaning through the chaos and pain. We typically do not ask, 'Where does suffering come from in the first place?' If you happen to believe that we have simply evolved from primordial goo that came alive billions of years ago, then you will not find any hope. The strong eating the weak—the 'survival of the fittest'—will lead you back to a remorseful conclusion: too bad.

Even with such a hopeless conclusion, however, you still want answers. You still want to be able to plant your feet on solid ground. That is what this brief guide is about. But you have a number of competing voices, all giving their 'insights' into the origin of suffering.

LOOKING FOR ANSWERS

The famed atheist Bertrand Russell believed that all human life—its origin, its development, and its suffering—is simply the product of *chance*. Life has no ultimate purpose and we hope in vain for the afterlife. He concluded, 'Only within the scaffolding of these truths, only on the firm foundation of unyielding despair, can the soul's habitation henceforth be safely built.'[1]

Unyielding despair? Is that really our 'foundation' and hope? At least Russell presents a consistent conclusion to atheism.

Or, you might end up with a view of suffering devoid of meaning. Take the more recent atheist, Richard Dawkins, who writes, 'The total amount of suffering per year in the natural world is beyond all decent contemplation… some people are going to get hurt, other people are going to get lucky, and you will not find any rhyme or reason in it.' He adds, 'The universe is…nothing but pitiless indifference.'[2] Jean-Paul Sartre, another avowed atheist, once mused that the only question he could not answer was why he did not commit suicide.[3]

Russell, Dawkins, and Sartre all admit the inevitable conclusions of their anti-God worldview—'unyielding despair' and 'pitiless indifference.' The English journalist, Steve Turner, was right when he explained this perspective with insightful clarity when he wrote:

> *If chance be*
> *the Father of all flesh,*
> *disaster is his rainbow in the sky,*
> *and when you hear:*
> *State of Emergency!*
> *Sniper Kills Ten!*
> *Troops on Rampage!*
> *Whites Go Looting!*
> *Bomb Blasts School!*
> *It is but the sound of man*
> *worshipping his maker.*

Anti-Christian worldviews and faith systems simply cannot provide answers to life's most basic questions, including those related to the experience of suffering.

When we turn to pop culture, it does not take long to see that it, too, lacks the helpful tools for understanding and responding to pain. Shock, hopelessness, and lofty platitudes often become the end result, which fail to provide true healing and hope. Unfortunately, even those who turn to the church for answers often find themselves disillusioned by *Your Best Life Now* or other self-help guides when their life is smashed against the rocks of affliction. Some Christians think they are *saints* in the hands of an angry God—that the 'man upstairs' is unjustly out to get them.

Jonathan Edwards (1703–1758) preached the famous sermon, 'Sinners in the Hands of an Angry God' in 1741. Edwards presented a God-centered view of the Christian life, which understood God to be self-sufficient and deserving of all glory. Such a high view of God necessarily puts our suffering in a proper perspective, seeing that we do not deserve health, wealth, and prosperity.

Because we feel *entitled* to health, wealth, and prosperity, our failure at achieving these things often leaves us empty and still dreaming. As singer-songwriter Laura Story has proposed in her award-winning song, 'Blessings,' we cannot imagine sufferings as God's 'mercies in disguise.' Yes, through the lens of Scripture, we can see how sufferings are displays of God's mercies. John Piper writes in *When the Darkness Will Not Lift*, 'We find ourselves… always thinking about the way to maximize our leisure and escape pressure.'[4] We feel that we deserve happiness and because we believe that happiness is attained only in the *absence* of affliction, we become like rudderless boats, lost at sea, when the storms of suffering blow against our bow. We lose course and often drift further and further away from the sunny sands of biblical truth.

But beyond the clichés and the 'pitiless indifference' of our anti-God culture, we *can* find understanding, hope, and how to respond to suffering in a God-honoring way.

That is what this book is about. But, first, we need to understand where suffering comes from.

THE FALL INTO SIN

As you look through the six days of creation in Genesis 1, you will notice that God did not create suffering. On the contrary, he created all things 'very good' (Gen. 1:31). He created the heavens above and the earth below. He created man—male and female—to live in perfect harmony with him and with one another. Significantly, the image of God instilled a reflection of God's relational character in the human heart.

When Adam and Eve were created, they did not possess the sin-nature that you and I have; they were free to obey or disobey God without a propensity toward evil. But as the Scriptures record, paradise was soon lost. Adam and Eve desired self-autonomy—a life *independent* of God—and ate of the forbidden fruit. Thereafter, 'every intention of the thoughts of [man's] heart was only evil continually' (Gen. 6:5). This is an important concept.

Have you ever had a grocery cart with a bad wheel? It is an extremely frustrating experience because it continually pulls the cart off course and—if you were to simply push it and let it go—it would smash into the food aisle. Your heart is like that bad wheel. You are bent toward sin every time *unless* your heart (the wheel) is changed by the sovereign grace of God. The apostle Paul makes this point clearly in Romans 3: 'None is righteous, no, not one; no one understands; no one seeks for God' (v. 10-11). Before God saved us, we were in rebellion against him.

The gravity and depth of Adam and Eve's sin was not so much in the act of eating the fruit, but in the act of sinning against a holy and righteous God. For example, there are far greater consequences to hitting the Queen of England than hitting a deacon in your church! It is the same act (hitting), but the position, power, authority, and dignity of the person against whom you act renders the offense (and thus the punishment) far greater. That is why eternal death is an appropriate consequence for sinning against an eternal and holy God. What God pronounced 'very good' at creation—those made in his image—turned on him in an act of cosmic treason.

Immediately, the blame game began: Adam blamed Eve, and Eve blamed Satan. Man's desire for the fruit of the forbidden tree ushered in the fruit of the Fall—what we call *suffering*.

SUFFERING: THE FRUIT OF THE FALL

God could have wiped Adam and Eve from the face of the earth at that point, and he would have been completely just in doing so. But he did not. Rather, he proclaimed a message of grace. God told the serpent, 'I will put enmity between you and the woman, and between your offspring and her offspring; he shall bruise your head, and you shall bruise his heel' (Gen. 3:15). God would fulfill his promise by sending a King to strike the deathblow to that 'ancient serpent' (Rev. 12:9).

Why would God be completely just in not saving anybody? What is it about our sin that deserves death and hell forever?

Despite the promise of grace, however, the curse of the Fall, including suffering, remained. Notice the word 'pain' in God's judgment to Adam and Eve. He said to the woman, 'I will surely multiply your *pain* in childbearing; in *pain* you shall bring forth children' and to the man, 'Cursed is the ground because of you; in *pain* you shall eat of it all the days of your life; thorns and thistles it shall bring forth for you' (v. 16-18, emphasis mine).

At the Fall, we see the introduction of pain, suffering, and even death as Adam was barred from the 'tree of life' (v. 24). The apostle Paul would later write, 'Just as sin came into the world through one man, and death through sin, so death spread to all men because all sinned' (Rom. 5:12). Adam represented the human race as our federal head and so his sin was credited (or imputed) to all born *of Adam*. Not only do we possess a sin nature from conception in the womb (Ps. 51:5), we come face-to-face with the stark reality, 'You were dead in your trespasses and sins...children of wrath, like the rest of mankind' (Eph. 2:1, 3).

The origin of suffering, therefore, is directly related to the Fall of mankind into sin. Various diseases, pain caused by the sin and wickedness of others, and the 'thorns and thistles' of this cursed creation—which is waiting to be set free from its bondage to decay (Rom. 8:21) when King Jesus will usher in the new heaven and the new earth

(Rev. 21:1)—became the new normal. Suffering, therefore, points us to the Fall of mankind and our rebellion against a holy God.

When we suffer today, it should point us to the depth of our sin and the abundance of God's grace in saving us through the shed blood of Jesus. But it should also point us back to where suffering began—in the garden. And as we consider the suffering and death brought about through the first Adam, we look to the life and joy brought about through the second Adam. This sin-filled, suffering-laden world provided the humble environment of the incarnate God. Jesus humbled himself and became obedient to death, even death on a cross. This would not have been needed or possible if it were not for the Fall, which initiated the reality and presence of suffering.

EXTERNAL, INTERNAL, AND SPIRITUAL SUFFERING

How should we understand the types of suffering we experience? Are some sufferings worse than others? It is helpful to understand something about the nature of the suffering itself and how it affects us in order to find healing. The writer of Hebrews presents an array of various sufferings among those who faced costly persecution:

Some were tortured...others suffered mocking and flogging, and even chains and imprisonment. They were stoned, they were sawn in two, they were killed with the sword. They went about in skins of sheep and goats, destitute, afflicted, mistreated (Heb. 11:35-37).

Maybe you have experienced some of these as well. The apostle Paul also listed a variety of sufferings he personally experienced:

> Five times I received at the hands of the Jews the forty lashes less one. Three times I was beaten with rods. Once I was stoned. Three times I was shipwrecked; a night and a day I was adrift at sea, on frequent journeys, in danger from rivers, danger from robbers, danger from my own people, danger from Gentiles, danger in the city, danger in the wilderness, danger at sea, danger from false brothers; in toil and hardship, through many a sleepless night, in hunger and thirst, often without food, in cold and exposure. And, apart from other things, there is the daily pressure on me of my anxiety for all the churches (2 Cor. 11:24-28).

You could imagine Paul being one walking piece of scar tissue. It is hard to imagine so much suffering for one person today, although it certainly exists in the world today.

For most people, *internal* sufferings—grief, despair, and sorrow (among others)—are far more painful than *external* sufferings: sickness, bodily pain, hunger, etc. Indeed, throughout history, many people have preferred to experience external suffering rather than bear the torments of internal pain. Moreover, external sufferings often bring about internal pain. For example, the death of a loved one (an external event) is one of life's greatest sorrows (an internal pain). A husband walking out on his wife and family (external event) would most certainly cause deep feelings of rejection and loneliness (internal pain). External afflictions can certainly leave their share of scars, but internal afflictions often leave lasting impressions, wounds, despair, and heart-scars.

In addition to external and internal sufferings, however, we need to understand a third category of affliction, *spiritual* suffering. Spiritual suffering can be brought about by satanic oppression, a deadness of faith, or a besetting sin in your life (e.g., an addiction). The later English puritan, John Flavel, writes, 'The least sin is more formidable to you than the greatest affliction: doubtless you would rather chuse [*sic*] to bury all your children, than provoke and grieve your heavenly Father.'[5] Flavel gets at the torments of spiritual affliction brought about by one's sin.

Sin that clings closely to your heart and finds continual expression in your life often leads to spiritual distress and, therefore, it can rob you of a healthy and hopeful perspective on your suffering. Moreover, Satan's *busy* time is our *suffering* time because he desires us to abandon the God we love and we are oftentimes spiritually weak when suffering most. The ancient serpent is still at work.

While Satan certainly works to take us from our love and knowledge of God, we are not to blame our sin on Satan. In other words, we are accountable and responsible for our own sin. God has given us his means of grace—his Word, prayer, and the sacraments—to fight for faith against the fiery darts of the devil. But we cannot shift the blame to him; we are to confess and repent of our own sin.

Can you see the connection between external, internal, and spiritual suffering in your life or in the life of someone you love? Can you pinpoint events in your past that continue to cause pain and hurt? These three types of suffering are often interwoven chords and can only be broken through the sovereign grace of God. That is what the rest of this book is really about.

Our great hope in the midst of suffering is not 'unyielding despair' or vain attempts to simply escape its dark reality, or even self-help theology, 'You can do it; God can help.' No, our great hope is anchored in our good and gracious God. He is self-sufficient—perfectly complete in himself from all eternity—as Father, Son, and Holy Spirit. He knows all things, commands all things, and will continue to make a great name for himself. But how do we reconcile God's sovereign and good character with the reality of suffering? How can these two truths coexist?

2

SUFFERING

AND THE SOVEREIGNTY OF GOD

When tragedy strikes—school shooting, hurricane, genocide—TV hosts and radio personalities, at least in the USA, frequently invite panels of religious 'experts' to answer the ever-present question: 'How can a good God allow bad things to happen?' Of course, atheists always seem to dodge the spotlight, as if they do not have to *also* give an account! The 'problem' of evil and suffering is one that *every* worldview and faith system must address if it is going to be relevant, consistent, and meaningful.

Christians, however, can take comfort in the fact that the Scriptures give a sustainable, coherent, helpful, and hopeful understanding of the connection between God's goodness, sovereignty, and omnipresence[6] on the one hand and the reality of suffering on the other: *God is good, sovereign, and everywhere at the same time.* If any one of these attributes of God is false or lacking, we cannot have a sustainable or consistent biblical view of suffering. Let me explain.

If God is good, but not sovereign, then he does not have enough control or power to stop suffering. While he might be benevolent and nice, he simply could not stop the suffering if he wanted. If God is sovereign, but not good, then he is simply a divine bully, wicked and unjust. If God were both sovereign and good, but was not everywhere at the same time by his Spirit, then he could not effectively exert his sovereignty and goodness wherever suffering occurs. Therefore, all three of these divine attributes must be true at the same time for a biblically *consistent* understanding of why and how God ordains suffering.

Christians and Jews wrestled with the realities of God's sovereignty and goodness after World War II and the holocaust, when over 6 million Jews were systematically killed. If God were in complete control, how could he have let such wickedness prevail? In the end, many abandoned the idea of God's absolute sovereignty in favor of God's goodness. Obviously, they did not see how the two attributes could 'fit' together.

GOD'S GOODNESS

That God is *good* refers to the fact that he is morally perfect—without evil or injustice—in his being and in all his actions. The prophet Nahum writes, 'The LORD is good, a stronghold in the day of trouble' (1:7). The Psalmist declares to God, 'You are good and do good' (119:68). There is not the slightest drop of corruption or immorality in the ocean of God's holiness: 'God is light, and in him is no darkness at all' (1 John 1:5).

God's goodness also assumes his moral holiness. Biblical 'holiness' primarily has to do with being *set apart*. But it also conveys a secondary meaning of moral perfection—the essence of all that is good. And if God is holy and good, he must also be just; he must right the wrongs and punish sin. Psalm 33:5 states, 'He loves righteousness and justice; the earth is full of the steadfast love of the LORD.' Again, that God is holy primarily means that he is wholly other, set apart as the Creator from his creation. But it also entails the truth that he is morally perfect and without a speck of evil.

Historically, most Christians, when suffering, find it easy to affirm God's goodness. Many are not willing to give up this attribute of God. It is his sovereignty on the other hand that most often comes into question.

GOD'S SOVEREIGNTY

God's sovereignty is one of his divine attributes that communicates his lordship and powerful rule over the universe. That God is 'Lord' means that he is all-powerful, possesses all authority, and is all present. As R. C. Sproul has often said, there is not one maverick molecule in all the universe that is outside the powerful reach and governing will of God. Not the tiniest worm, the fiercest tornado, or the wisest thought is outside the immediate and eternal control of God.

God's sovereignty is expressed or displayed in two interrelated ways. First, God's sovereignty is expressed in his *eternal decrees*. God's decrees are his set plan for all that happens. Before you simply cast this doctrine aside as fatalism or impersonal determinism, please follow this closely. The prophet Isaiah records:

> For I am God, and there is no other; I am God, and there is none like me, declaring the end from the beginning and from ancient times things not yet done, saying, 'My counsel shall stand, and I will accomplish all my purpose,' calling a bird of prey from the east, the man of my counsel from a far country. I have spoken, and I will bring it to pass; I have purposed, and I will do it (Isa. 46:9-11).

All things come to pass 'according to the purpose of him who works *all things* according to the counsel of his will' (Eph. 1:11, emphasis mine). He plans the course of history that he might be glorified.

God's decrees also include all of his promises we find throughout Scripture. In fact, *if God were not sovereign, we could not trust his promises!* Why? Because if something were beyond God's control, it could potentially disrupt and thwart his sovereign plans. It would be like the sand granule in the machine. But this is not the God we trust. The true and living God has declared the end from the beginning. Even the death of Jesus was 'Plan A,' as the apostle Peter preached: 'This Jesus, delivered up according to the definite plan and foreknowledge of God, you crucified and killed by the hands of lawless men' (Acts 2:23).

The events and realities that we find in the book of Revelation comprise the predetermined will of God. Are those events mere suggestions or God's well-wishes? Certainly not. They will come to pass because they are part of his sovereign decree. When the apostle John looked around and no one was worthy to open the scroll with the seven seals, he began to weep. But then, one of the elders said to him, 'Weep no more; behold, the Lion of the tribe of Judah, the Root of David, has conquered, so that he can open the scroll and its seven seals' (Rev. 5:5). The Lamb slain from before the foundation of the world (Rev. 13:8)—as it were in God's eternal perspective— took the scroll to execute the Father's sovereign plan and decrees through the ages. The Lamb's 'book of life' also bears witness to this reality. So God's sovereignty is expressed or displayed by his eternal decrees.

The second way in which God's sovereignty is expressed is in his day-to-day *providence*. 'Providence' refers to God's eternal decrees *in action*, the practical outworking of God's sovereign control. For example, let us say God predestined Lydia to be saved from before the foundation of the world (Eph. 1:4-5). That would be an expression of God's *decree*. But one sunny July day, Lydia believes on the Lord Jesus for salvation—in real time and space—when she hears the gospel preached (cf. Acts 16:14). This would be according to God's *providence*.

Of course, God's decrees and his providence are two sides of the same coin; they both are expressions of his sovereignty. In fact, not even a sparrow falls to the ground apart from the sovereign will of God (Matt. 10:29).

This is why we can talk about God 'governing' all things. To *govern* was an old English sailor's term. It was used to describe all of the moving parts and mechanisms to steer the course of the ship from point A to point B. In a similar way, God governs all the events and mechanisms to steer the course of history across the sea of time, until it reaches the sunny sands of his appointed end.

Why does this matter? For one, people usually attack God's sovereignty first when bad things happen. They can affirm his goodness, but do not seem to like the fact that he is also sovereign. But Scripture is crystal clear: all things, all events, all history, and all salvation come to pass according to the sovereign will of God—*suffering included*. But we need to understand a bit more about the nature of suffering to bring this idea full circle.

SUFFERING AND 'EVIL'

Suffering—in and of itself—is not morally evil. Typically, the two are linked together, but this can lead to a misunderstanding. As we have seen, suffering is the fruit

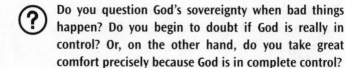

Do you question God's sovereignty when bad things happen? Do you begin to doubt if God is really in control? Or, on the other hand, do you take great comfort precisely because God is in complete control?

or curse of the Fall. Moral evil, on the other hand, is that which rebels against God and his will. Thus, *suffering is the curse of evil, not evil itself.* It would be rather odd (unbiblical?) for Paul to say, for example, 'We rejoice in our sufferings' (Rom. 5:3) if suffering were evil!

Therefore, God can ordain suffering and keep his goodness intact. He does not sovereignly create evil. He can ordain suffering, but he is not the author of sin and evil. So how does God's character connect with the reality of evil in the world? Answer: *God permits evil, restraints evil, and overrules evil for his good and sovereign purposes.*[7] Let us look briefly at these three actions of God in relation to evil by way of a few biblical examples.

Remember the story of Job where God asked Satan, 'Have you considered my servant Job' (Job 1:8)? We are told that Job was a blameless and upright man, who feared God and turned away from evil (v. 8). Satan desired to bring pain and ruin upon Job, but he could only exert his malicious intent by the *permission* of God. God limited Satan's evil activity by permitting Satan to do harm. Even Satan is on a sovereign leash. In 2 Corinthians 12, Paul relates his 'thorn in the flesh' as something intended by God to keep him humble, but he calls it 'a messenger of Satan' (v. 7). You see, God permits Satanic activity for much greater purposes.

But God not only permits evil, he also *restrains* evil. For example, we read of Abraham's journey toward the Negeb in Genesis 20. When he and his wife, Sarah, came to the region of Gerar, Abimelech—the king of Gerar— took notice of Sarah and sought her as his wife. Abraham lied and told him that she was his sister and so Abimelech took her to lie with her. But before he committed adultery by sleeping with Sarah, God told Abimelech, 'You are a dead man because of the woman whom you have taken, for she is a man's wife' (v. 3). Abimelech pleaded to God for mercy because he did not know Sarah was Abraham's wife. So God told Abimelech: 'I know that you have done this in the integrity of your heart, and *it was I who kept you from sinning against me.* Therefore I did not let you touch her' (v. 6, emphasis mine). God sovereignly restrained further sin and evil for his good purposes. Apart from his common grace in our everyday lives, restraining sin, we would spin headlong into further self-destruction and suffering.

But God not only permits and restrains evil, he also *overrules* it for good. One of the clearest examples of this is found in the account of Joseph and his brothers. Because of their jealousy of their father's love for Joseph, his brothers sold him into slavery. Potiphar, the captain of Pharaoh's guard, bought Joseph and, over time, made him manager over his house. But Potiphar's wife sought Joseph to lay with her and, one day, while being assaulted by her desires, Joseph ran—leaving his cloak behind in the clutches of the woman.

She screamed and lied to Potiphar's men, telling them that Joseph had tried to rape her and so Joseph was thrown into prison. Through a series of events, Joseph correctly interpreted Pharaoh's dreams and was made second in command over all of Egypt. After seven years of plenty, the region faced seven years of famine. By God's grace,

Joseph had ordered extra grain to be saved during the seven years of plenty and so people came from near and far to purchase grain from the Egyptians.

In time, Joseph's brothers also came to purchase grain. After several encounters with his brothers—who did not recognize him—Joseph finally disclosed his identity. They felt terribly sorry for their actions. But Joseph told them, 'As for you, you meant evil against me, but God meant it for good, to bring it about that many people should be kept alive, as they are today' (Gen. 50:20).

While Joseph's brothers meant harm and evil against Joseph, God *overruled* their evil intent, bringing their wicked desires into the fold of his eternal and sovereign purposes. The apostle Paul echoes this when he wrote, 'And we know that for those who love God *all things* work together for good, for those who are called according to his purpose' (Rom. 8:28, emphasis mine).

Because we are finite and our minds are limited as God's created image-bearers, we have been given only what we need to know and understand in God's Word. Indeed, 'The secret things belong to the LORD our God,

A modern heretical theological position, oftentimes called Open Theism, suggests that God's foreknowledge and providence are open to change. In this view, God took a big risk in allowing Adam and Eve to fall into sin. He also took a big risk in sending his Son to die on the cross—Jesus died in hopes that people might be saved, but God is not in control of that. Open Theism affirms that God's decisions are dependent upon man's decisions, not the other way around. Some of the major proponents of Open Theism include Gregory Boyd, Clark Pinnock, and John E. Sanders.

but the things that are revealed belong to us and to our children forever' (Deut. 29:29). Again, while suffering is not morally evil, God permits, restrains, and overrules evil for his good and sovereign purposes.

GOD'S SOVEREIGNTY AND 'SECONDARY CAUSES'

Deism, the belief that God created the world only to sit back and watch it all play out on its own—apart from his providential governing—gained popularity in the seventeenth and eighteenth centuries. This idea oftentimes presents God as a divine clock-maker: he simply winds up the clock (with its pre-established 'laws of nature') and lets it go.

This, however, is *not* the biblical view of creation or of God's sovereignty. The Puritan, Thomas Watson, once warned that we should not devalue a high view of God's immediate care of his creation, 'as if [God] sat in heaven, and minded not of what became of things here below; like a man that makes a clock and then leaves it to go off itself.'[8] Indeed, the Reformers and Puritans believed that the world 'was not a machine that ran automatically according to an initial plan.'[9] Rather, God created the world and subsequently governs his creation by his day-to-day providence.

While God certainly created both the visible world and the invisible 'laws' of creation (gravity, cause/effect, motion, weather patterns, etc.), he does not simply let those laws function apart from his immediate and providential ordering. In theological language, we call this the doctrine of *concurrence*—he concurrently establishes secondary causes in nature and providentially governs them at every second. Hurricanes, forest fires, and deadly floods all occur according to God's sovereign hand. Examples abound in the Scriptures. God caused the flood in Noah's day (Gen. 6-8). He sends the rain on both the just and the unjust (Matt. 5:45). As Elihu proclaims:

> For to the snow [God] says, 'Fall on the earth,' likewise to the downpour, his mighty downpour….By the breath of God, ice is given, and the broad waters are frozen fast. He loads the thick clouds with moisture; and the clouds scatter his lightning. They turn around and around by his guidance to accomplish all that he commands them on the face of the habitable world. Whether for correction or for his land or for love, *he causes it to happen* (Job 37:6-13, emphasis mine).

Read those last lines again. God *causes* even the seemingly 'natural' events to happen 'to accomplish all that he commands them on the face of the habitable world.' God does not come alongside the secondary laws of nature collaterally and on the bye. No, the secondary causes of nature exist and function only by the sovereign direction of God—every movement of the clouds, every falling sparrow, every flash of lightning.

IS MAN RESPONSIBLE?

With so much on God's sovereignty, you might be wondering about man's responsibility. Is God absolutely sovereign? Yes. Is man responsible? Yes. The Bible teaches that while God is sovereign, man is responsible for his actions and obedience to God. The Bible does *not* teach an abstract, impersonal, fatalism, but the personal providence of God—permitting, restraining, governing, overruling, and ordering 'all his creatures and all their actions.'[10]

The ancient Stoic philosophers envisioned a world in which we are like dogs, tied to a heavy cart rolling down a steep hill. You have no responsibility, no decision, and you are tied to an inanimate, impersonal course of events. This, of course, is not biblical. While God has decreed the end from the beginning, man is fully responsible. Prior to salvation, people do not have a 'free will,' as they are in bondage to sin, choosing rebellion against God every moment (whether they realize it or not). But by God's grace, he gives you a new heart, a freed will, to respond to him with loving faith.

Paul writes of both God's sovereignty and mans' responsibility in Philippians 2: 'Work out your own salvation with fear and trembling [man's responsibility], for it is God who works in you, both to will and to work for his good pleasure [God's sovereignty]' (v. 12-13). But because God's sovereignty is so often misunderstood in our day, we have taken some extended space to explore it in Scripture. God creates and rules everything as the Lord of the universe for his sovereign purposes. As the writer of Proverbs teaches, 'The LORD has made everything for its purpose, even the wicked for the day of trouble' (Prov. 16:4). Later, he adds, 'The heart of man plans his way,

SUFFERING AND THE SOVEREIGNTY OF GOD | 25

but the Lord establishes his steps' (Prov. 16:9) and 'The lot is cast into the lap, but its every decision is from the LORD' (v. 33).

Thus, to summarize our answer to the question: 'Does God sovereignly ordain suffering?' Answer: 'Yes.' God powerfully, authoritatively, decretally, and effectually ordains suffering. *But why?* We will look at the answer to that question in the next chapter.

God is sovereign and man is responsible. Both are clearly taught in Scripture. This does not mean, however, that man contributes to his salvation in any way. Because man is, by nature, born into sin, considered dead in his trespasses and sins, he is in bondage and, therefore, he doesn't have 'free will.' God's Spirit frees us by causing us to be born again. In no way, does this contradict or detract from God's sovereignty or from man's responsibility.

3

WHY DOES GOD ORDAIN SUFFERING?

As we have seen, God is both completely good and completely sovereign over all things, all events, and all suffering. All things work together for the ultimate good of those who love God and are called according to his purpose (Rom. 8:28). But *why* does God allow suffering? What are his purposes in ordaining suffering?

THE 'MYSTERY' OF PROVIDENCE

God's providence works in relation to and in concurrence with his revealed Word, the Bible, because the two flow from the same Fountainhead. God's revealed decrees in time and space (i.e., his providence) and his revealed

Word work together in a harmonious tapestry of wisdom, design, and purpose. Thus, our experience of suffering should be interpreted through the lens of Scripture; otherwise, it will remain to us purposeless, pointless, and hopeless. Any insight or understanding, therefore, of God's design in our suffering should dovetail and echo the truth of his Word. The Scriptures navigate us like a compass in our course through this world of pain and suffering.

We must be careful, however, not to *over*-read God's intentions into our afflictions. Happiness and prosperity are not necessarily signs of God's approval or blessing. Conversely, suffering and affliction are not necessarily signs of God's disapproval or judgment. We see the saints of old complaining of this apparent irony:

'Why do the wicked live, reach old age, and grow mighty in power? They spend their days in prosperity, and in peace they go down to Sheol' (Job 21:7, 13).

'Evildoers not only prosper but they put God to the test and they escape' (Mal. 3:15).

'For I was envious of the arrogant, when I saw the prosperity of the wicked. For they have no pangs until death; their bodies are fat and sleek. Behold, these are the wicked; always at ease, they increase in riches' (Ps. 73:3-4, 12).

We must be cautious, therefore, in how we 'assign' specific comforts or afflictions with God's providential blessing or judgment. For example, if you contract cancer, you should not say, 'If only I had given a bigger tithe to my church or had not spoken harshly to my teenage son, then I wouldn't have cancer.' That is making God contingent upon us, as if he owes us health, wealth, and prosperity in response to our good deeds.

Even though all events (suffering included) are the result of God's sovereign plan, only God knows the ultimate meaning and purpose behind those events. Thus, we cannot escape the reality that God's manifold purposes in our suffering will remain somewhat mysterious. The mystery of God's providence, therefore, lies not in the fact that God ordains suffering, but rather *why* He ordains suffering at specific times and in specific places. Be that as it may, Scripture does give us some instruction and insight into why God ordains suffering, for both his people and the unbelieving world.

It's easy to fall into the trap of assuming that we know why God sends specific sufferings or blessings. When might people try to do this?

THE BIG PICTURE

God ordains suffering ultimately for his glory, the good of his people, and the judgment of the unbelieving world. These are the overarching purposes of God in ordaining suffering. The apostle Paul writes, 'For from him and through him and to him are *all things*. To him be glory forever' (Rom. 11:36, emphasis mine). The apostle John records the heavenly throng, 'Worthy are you, our

Lord and God, to receive glory and honor and power' (Rev. 4:11). We see that same expression by Job, after hearing of his children's death: 'The LORD gave, and the LORD has taken away; blessed be the name of the LORD' (Job 1:21). Paul elsewhere teaches, 'All things were created through [Jesus] and for him...that in everything he might be preeminent' (Col. 1:16-18). In a discussion on God's design in our suffering, Peter encourages his readers by pointing them to the great end of their earthly pilgrimage: 'that in everything God may be glorified through Jesus Christ. To him belong glory and dominion forever and ever' (1 Pet. 4:11).

God's glory, then, is his ultimate purpose for all things and he expresses his glory through the suffering of his saints and the unbelieving world, albeit for very different reasons. We will take the remainder of the chapter to look at why God ordains suffering for his people, we need to understand what differentiates between the purpose and intention of God's suffering for the Christian and the non-Christian.

Those who have been born again by the Holy Spirit, forgiven of their sins through the shed blood of Christ, and justified through Christ's righteousness imputed to their account and received by faith alone are no longer under the condemnation of God (Rom. 8:1). Their afflictions come to them not as God's vindictive wrath, but as his fatherly discipline because it is only through Christ's meritorious blood that affliction turns to blessing.

For the unbeliever, however, suffering comes as raw effects of God's just wrath for sin—*partly* in this life and *fully* in the life to come. Sufferings of this life serve as warnings of the greater suffering beyond the grave. Because God's wrath has not been poured out on his Son on their behalf, it is poured out on them.

Jesus experienced hell for his sheep, his 'bride,' the church. This is what the Apostle's Creed means when it says, 'And he descended into hell.' Jesus descended into the agony and full judgment of God on behalf of his elect. Because of this, believers will never experience the wrath of God in judgment, but rather paternal displeasure in discipline.

WHY GOD ORDAINS SUFFERING FOR HIS PEOPLE

If you have trusted in Christ as the Savior and Lord of your life, you can rest in the truth that your afflictions and sufferings come to you for your ultimate good and God's ultimate glory. But let us look at five specific biblical reasons why God ordains suffering for his people.[11]

To Kill Sin and Produce Godliness

To kill (or 'mortify') sin, God uses suffering to reveal to us the sin that clings so closely to our hearts. When we suddenly bear an affliction, our pride, impatience, and unbelief will oftentimes surface. Suffering breaks open the sinful heart, laying it bare and visible. When I have faced suffering in my life, I have responded with anger and impatience. The suffering itself is not evil, but it shows me the sin still present in my heart. Sometimes, my suffering reveals my lack of faith in God's promises.

I begin questioning God, 'How could you let this happen?' Again, the suffering seeks and finds my sin so that I might see it, confess it, repent of it, and trust in the gospel of grace.

Suffering also can deter me from greater sin. For example, the internal shame and torment of being 'found out' that I have gossiped about somebody will often deter me from gossiping. For some, the greater fear of suffering in prison deters them from committing the crime in the first place. You see, the consequences of our sin— oftentimes falling under the banner of 'suffering'—can be enough to prevent us from continuing in that sin.

By these means, God uses suffering to mortify our sin. If we are prone to love something in this world— house, spouse, children, job, etc.—*more* than God, he will sometimes remove the 'idol,' which will cause pain and suffering. But, in doing so, we are freed to refocus our primary love on God. King David saw a beautiful woman bathing and sent for her. After committing adultery, he had her husband killed on the battlefield. The prophet Nathan confronted him about his sin and David responded with Psalm 51, where we find these words:

> Have mercy on me, O God, according to your steadfast love;
> according to your abundant mercy blot out my transgressions.
> Wash me thoroughly from my iniquity, and cleanse me from
> my sin! Let the bones that you have broken rejoice. Hide
> your face from my sins, and blot out all my iniquities. Create
> in me a clean heart, O God, and renew a right spirit within
> me (Ps. 51:1-2, 8-10).

Suffering serves as a cleanser, revealing to us our sin, deterring us from greater sin, and mortifying that sin in the process.

The flip side of God killing our sin is God producing in us greater godliness—whereby we are made more and more into the image of Christ. This is what we call *sanctification*—'the work of God's grace whereby we are renewed in the whole man after the image of God, and are enabled more and more to die unto sin, and to live unto righteousness.'[12] God will also use the community of the church to spur one another on and be the context where iron sharpens iron (Prov. 27:17). When affliction falls upon a community of believers, they are brought together in a greater bond and union. They can strengthen and support each other, leading to greater growth as followers of Christ. Thus, God uses suffering to both kill sin and produce greater godliness.

To Relinquish the Temporal for the Eternal

God also uses suffering to wean us from a love of this world and redirect our thoughts and affections for that which is eternal: 'Set your minds on things that are above, not on things that are on earth' (Col. 3:2). Jesus told the rich young ruler to sell all that he had and give it to the poor. Then, he said, you will have treasure in heaven. The young man went away sorrowful. Sometimes, God will simply take those treasures away for our greater good—it is better to lose an eye than for your whole body to be thrown into hell (Matt. 5:29).

As Christians, the afflictions we experience in this life should point us to the reality that we are 'sojourners and exiles' (1 Pet. 2:11) here on earth, journeying toward the celestial city. We are 'strangers and exiles' (Heb. 11:13) and 'our citizenship is in heaven' (Phil. 3:20). This world is not our home and the afflictions we experience along the way serve as directional arrows directing us to relinquish our hold on the fading things of this world and lay hold of that which is eternal and honoring to God.

Sometimes, we cling too tightly to that which withers and fades away—'where moth and rust destroy and where thieves break in and steal' (Matt. 6:19). But God is our greatest Treasure and he may use suffering to break our earthly treasures so that (as the old hymn says) 'the things of this earth will grow strangely dim in the light of his glory and grace.' If God is your greatest Treasure and Refuge, come what may. He proves himself as our chief Comfort especially in seasons of suffering. Flavel writes,

> My name is blotted out of the earth, but still it is written in heaven. God hath taken my only son from me, but he hath given his only Son for me, and to me. He hath broken off my hopes and expectations as to this world, but my hopes of heaven are fixed sure and immoveable forever. My house and heart are both in confusion and great disorder, but I have still an everlasting covenant, ordered in all things, and sure.[13]

Paul writes that the 'God of all comfort…comforts us in all our afflictions' (2 Cor. 1:3-4). He adds, 'For as we share abundantly in Christ's sufferings, so through Christ we share abundantly in comfort too' (v. 5). As the God of true comfort, we are to see our present sufferings 'preparing us for an eternal weight of glory beyond all comparison' (2 Cor. 4:17).

To Produce a Sincere Faith, Devoid of Hypocrisy

The third reason God may use suffering is to refine us, like fire refining gold by removing the dross (Jer. 9:7; Zech. 13:9; Mal. 3:3). Suffering will often distinguish the true believer from the hypocrite by the response of each. In our suffering, we are given the opportunity to discover the sincerity of our love, hope, and faith in God.

Are there areas of dishonesty or insincerity? A plunge into a season of affliction can reveal these. When suffering falls on a church—whether through illness or persecution—'Christ's summer friends' flee.[14] Affliction causes the believer to cling to God and the unbeliever to forsake him. In this way, it comes as a sort of test or trial to separate the sheep and goats and to refine his precious people through the fire. Having a sincere faith in the promises of God also produces greater *assurance* of salvation, which the Reformers called heaven on earth.

To Bear Witness to the World

Under the rod of affliction, we are given opportunity to bear witness to the reality of the power of the gospel in our lives—which effectively calls others to repent and believe the gospel. When a Christian faces suffering, the unbelieving world has opportunity to see the sincerity and reality of the power of God to transform his or her *perspective* of and *response* to that suffering, and thus it serves as a witness of the gospel's reality and truth. In other words, the believer's own endurance under trial serves as a great witness to the truth of God's Word.

I have known believers who have suffered well and unbelieving onlookers taking particular note and inquiring as to the unshakable hope and inner peace the sufferer enjoys. God uses the suffering of his people to show his remarkable grace in securing their eternal salvation. Our frequent trials prove that our hope and faith is not in vain, but rather serve as a wonderful occasion to demonstrate the reality of the gospel.

To Cultivate Fellowship with God through his Word, Prayer, and Sacrament

The prophet Hosea records, 'Come, let us return to the LORD; for he has torn us, that he may heal us; he has struck us down, that he will bind us up' (Hos. 6:1). Indeed, as we experience suffering at the sovereign and loving hand of God, we are to cultivate communion and fellowship with Jesus Christ, the greatest Sufferer. In this way, we 'share his sufferings' (Phil. 3:10). This was the apostle Peter's instruction: 'Do not be surprised at the fiery trial when it comes upon you to test you, as though something strange were happening to you. But rejoice insofar as you share Christ's sufferings' (1 Pet. 4:12-13). He adds, 'Let those who suffer according to God's will entrust their souls to a faithful Creator' (v. 19).

When we experience suffering, we are driven to cling
to our Rock, Refuge, and Fortress—the true and living
God. Indeed, 'God is our refuge and strength, a very
present help in trouble' (Ps. 46:1). How do we practically
go about entrusting ourselves and cultivating communion
with God under trial? We do this ordinarily through his
Word, through prayer, and through the sacrament of the
Lord's Supper.

The Westminster Larger Catechism (1647) asks the question, 'What are the
outward means whereby Christ communicates to us the benefits of his
mediation?' Answer: 'The outward and ordinary means whereby Christ
communicates to his church the benefits of his mediation, are all his
ordinances; especially the word, sacraments, and prayer; all which are
made effectual to the elect for their salvation' (Q. 154).

God's Word is a lamp unto our feet and a light unto
our path (Ps. 119:105)—*especially* in times of suffering—
because its truth resonates with our renewed and
regenerated hearts. It is in the Scriptures that we can cast
our anchor when we feel tossed to and fro by the winds
of affliction. Nothing penetrates the darkness of pain like
the light of God's Word. In the Bible, God my Shepherd
leads me to the still waters and restores my soul. When
you are at a loss for words, let his Word become yours.
When we read, study, meditate, and memorize Scripture
during times of distress, it serves as a healing balm and
bread of life.

Prayer, too, becomes a pathway to communion with
God in seasons of suffering. Affliction has a way of
driving us to our knees in deep, frequent, and fervent

prayer. Communion with God through prayer—even letting God's words become your words uttered back to him—helps put the suffering in its proper perspective, under the sovereign grace of God.

Prayer is a means by which God communes with us and cultivates greater faith and assurance in his loving care even in difficult pain. Prayer is also a means whereby we experience that he is *with us* as our great Immanuel: 'Even though I walk through the valley of the shadow of death, I will fear no evil, for you are with me' (Ps. 23:4).

Finally, God ordains suffering to draw us into greater communion with himself through the sacrament of the Lord's Supper. In Communion, we do not merely think about Jesus suffering in our place; we actually *commune* with him really, truly, and spiritually by faith. He nourishes us and strengthens us, which is a wonderful remedy to the inner distress and despair oftentimes brought about by suffering.

Indeed, we commune with the Christ who drank the cup of suffering to its bitter end, so that we might share in his cup of blessing, which runs over. Our Suffering Servant knows our pains, trials, and afflictions because he experienced them and even more so: 'For we do not have a high priest who is unable to sympathize with our weaknesses, but one who in every respect has been tempted as we are, yet without sin' (Heb. 4:15).

As our heavenly Father, God sovereignly ordains suffering for his children as paternal discipline *because* he loves us (Heb. 12:6). He is weaning us from a love of this world, transforming us by the renewing of our minds (Rom. 12:2), and will complete that good work that he began in us for his glory (Phil. 1:6). May we rest in the surety of his covenant promises that, in the midst of suffering and trial, he will never leave us nor forsake us (Heb. 13:5).

4

HOW TO RIGHTLY RESPOND

DURING SUFFERING

When you experience suffering as a Christian, how do you typically respond? Perhaps with patience, fear, or despair? Some lash out in anger while others sink into an isolated depression. Still others joyfully accept what comes their way. But how *should* we respond when we experience suffering? It's a good question.

RESPONDING 'RIGHTLY' TO SUFFERING

Satan's busiest times seem to be our suffering times. When we come under external attacks of affliction and pain, it often brings out the internal attacks of temptation to sin. While this might seem unsympathetic and harsh at first mention, here's the truth: *Suffering does not give us a justifying excuse to sin.* In fact, sin actually increases the pain experienced. While it might seem medicinal to 'vent' in anger, binge on life-altering drugs or alcohol, and assume a full victimization mentality, these responses lead to greater internal suffering; they end up hurting us. Thus, we need to have a clear understanding of the 'right' responses during times of suffering.

First, and foremost, we see in Jesus the greatest example on how to respond amidst pain and affliction. The apostle Peter encourages us to look to Christ's example when he suffered. He writes,

> He committed no sin, neither was deceit found in his mouth. When he was reviled, he did not revile in return; when he suffered, he did not threaten, but continued entrusting himself to him who judges justly. Do not repay evil for evil or reviling for reviling, but on the contrary, bless, for to this you have been called, that you may obtain a blessing (1 Pet. 2:22-23; 3:9).

Peter adds later, in chapter 3, 'For it is better to suffer for doing good, if that should be God's will, than for doing evil' (v. 17) and in chapter 4, 'Let those who suffer according to God's will entrust their souls to a faithful Creator while doing good' (v. 19). We see here that God not only ordains suffering, but that we are to respond by 'doing good.' As anybody must learn about and prepare for marriage, for a new job, or for just about anything, so you must also learn about and prepare for suffering *so that* we might glorify God when under trial.

One common way that we sin during times of suffering is by showing *excessive* sorrow or hopeless despair. When we lose a loved one, we are not to grieve as those who have no hope (1 Thess. 4:13). In my years of pastoral ministry, I have witnessed on a number of occasions professing Christians become addicted to—and take advantage of—other peoples' generosity. They become the chronic victim and the whole world starts to revolve around them. They become more and more self-absorbed, which is a dead-end road. Why? Because you cannot find hope and healing when you are self-absorbed, no matter the pain and suffering you have experienced. Hope and healing come from God, not your heart. How we respond during times of suffering is important for actually healing and, thus, we should prepare to suffer rightly.

It is easy to become so overwhelmed while suffering that we can't think of others' needs. In other words, we oftentimes sin by becoming so self-centered, selfish, and a drain to others' generosity. Rather than consistently turning all of the attention to us, we need to remain sensitive to others' needs as well.

PREPARING TO SUFFER

Jesus often prepared his disciples to suffer and the apostles prepared their readers to suffer—so that they would be ready when the time came to give glory to God. In the Sermon on the Mount, Jesus tells his disciples,

> Blessed are those who are persecuted for righteousness' sake,
> for theirs is the kingdom of heaven. Blessed are you when
> others revile you and persecute you and utter all kinds of
> evil against you falsely on my account. Rejoice and be glad,
> for your reward is great in heaven, for so they persecuted the
> prophets who were before you (Matt. 5:10-12).

Much of Jesus' teaching actually involves preparing his
disciples to suffer, and how they should respond. 'In
this world,' Jesus says, 'you will have tribulation. But
take heart; I have overcome the world' (John 16:33). He
told Peter how Peter would die—by stretching out his
hands (Peter was later crucified upside down, with arms
stretched out). John comments on this, 'This [Jesus] said
to show by what kind of death [Peter] was to glorify God'
(John 21:19). Similarly, the New Testament epistles also
prepare Christians to suffering rightly. Space does not
permit me here to go through these, but even a cursory
scan reveals this to be the case.[15]

AFFIRMING GOD'S CHARACTER

Whether you are preparing to suffer or you are currently
suffering, it is important to affirm God's character at the
outset. In a culture and society that regularly disregards
the biblical revelation of God in general and during times
of suffering, in particular, we need to reclaim a solid and
unashamed affirmation of the true and living God. One
of the reasons for this is that a right understanding of

God's character has a direct impact on how we respond when we experience suffering.

That God is *sovereign* (as we have seen) provides a solid foundation of hope that whatever befalls us is according to his plan. Nothing can happen to us apart from his omnipotent hand. This is perhaps one of the greatest assurances of comfort and security. Many sufferers that I have known throughout the years find the sovereignty of God to be the most comforting aspect of God's character. They know that he is in control, no matter what befalls them.

That God is *eternal* gives us a big-picture perspective that we will get through our trials and one day enter into our heavenly rest. The suffering we experience is only temporary—this 'momentary affliction preparing us for an eternal weight of glory beyond all comparison' (2 Cor. 4:17). Thus, our afflictions are temporary. They might be severe, but they will not last forever.

That God is *wise* provides us with the assurance that even though we may not understand or see why we are suffering, we know that it is for our good and has come at just the right time and in just the right way. Our suffering is not arbitrary or random; it is purposeful and intentional. It is an important thread in the tapestry of God's manifold wisdom. As God tells Isaiah, 'For my thoughts are not your thoughts, neither are your ways my ways, declares the LORD. For as the heavens are higher than the earth, so are my ways higher than your ways and my thoughts higher than your thoughts' (Isa. 55:8-9).

I am very grateful that our God is all-wise and that all suffering is part of his wise plan for us.

That God is *good* reminds us that what we experience is not from a capricious, spiteful, or evil force, but from One who is wholly righteous and morally perfect. Your suffering comes from the ultimate source of Good himself. 'God is light, and in him is no darkness at all' (1 John 1:5). He alone sets the standard for what is good and true. Thus, our understanding of what is 'good' should continually be conformed to his standard so that we might be transformed by the renewing of our minds (Rom. 12:2).

That God is *omnipresent* (everywhere present) means that we can call upon him because he is near. He is never so far away that he is not with us. He is our *Immanuel*—God with us—and is with you right now. And, if you are one of his redeemed children, he is with you in an unbreakable covenant relationship—nothing and no one can snatch you out of his hand (John 10:29).

In order to respond rightly to God during suffering, we must *know* the God to whom we respond. A biblical and saving knowledge of God, therefore, is the first step in responding rightly to God when you face various afflictions.

PASSIVE RESPONSES

So what might a *right* response to suffering look like? A sufferer can rightly respond to suffering in one of two (or both) big-picture ways: with *passive* responses and *active* responses. Passive responses have to do with humbly accepting God's character (as presented above) and trusting him and his plan for your life. This response is not signified by much outward change in your behavior. Rather, it usually expresses itself in a quiet disposition, thoughtful meditation, enduring suffering with patience, and humble submission to the King of kings and the Lord of lords—who also happens to be our heavenly Father who loves us through his Son, Jesus.

Usually, these passive responses give way to active responses. That is, when you meditate upon God's character, cultivate patience, and joyfully submit to the will of God while suffering, your desire will often translate into actual outward expressions that *complete* your God-glorifying response. So what are some of these outward, active responses?

ACTIVE RESPONSES

Rather than sulking in endless misery, we are called to actively *improve* our sufferings for profitable gain. Afflictions are made profitable to us when we draw near to God in them.

Some of these active responses might include: (1) communing with God by reading and meditating upon his Word, (2) individual and corporate prayer, (3) resting in the assurance of his promises through the Lord's Supper, (4) reading helpful literature on the subject, (5) repenting of any particular sin that has become evident during your trial, (6) serving others as a follower of the Suffering Servant, (7) and intentional fellowship in your local church through corporate worship, small groups, or discipleship.

Both passive and active responses provide the sufferer with the added benefit of true healing. When we respond rightly during times of suffering, we also find healing. While getting drunk, bursting out in fits of anger, or taking on the chronic 'victim mentality' might *seem* to help ease the pain, in the end it only intensifies it. However, when we respond with faith, hope, and loving trust during times of suffering—passively and actively— we find healing and balm for our pain. In other words (and it is worth repeating) our sin during times of suffering intensifies the pain we experience while God's preserving grace to sustain us in times of suffering alleviates the pain we experience.

Horatio Spafford (1828–1888) experienced a string of afflictions. In 1870, his only son died from Scarlet Fever. The next year, the Great Chicago Fire rendered him destitute. Then, in an effort to regain financial stability, he made plans to travel to Europe. Because of unforeseen circumstances, he sent his family ahead of him on the SS Ville du Havre. While crossing the Atlantic, the ship hit another ship and sank. All four of his daughters died. As Spafford traveled across the Atlantic to meet his grieving wife, he passed near the location of his daughters' deaths and penned the words to the now-famous hymn—'It Is Well With My Soul'—When peace like a river attendeth my way; when sorrows like sea billows roll; whatever my lot, thou hast taught me to say, 'It is well, it is well with my soul.'

ASSURANCE: HEAVEN ON EARTH

Assurance of God's love for us in our salvation comes as a reward of God-honoring faith and availing ourselves of those means that God has ordained to assure us of his saving love during times of suffering. Thomas Watson, the well-known English Puritan, wrote, 'He that hath assurance can rejoice in tribulation; he can gather grapes from thorns, and honey out of the lion's carcass.'[16] Having assurance of God's eternal love for you is one of the most comforting joys you can experience—*a heaven on earth*!

Assurance of saving faith is distinct from the actual saving faith itself. Practically, this means that you can have seasons of doubt, regarding your salvation, but you can still have the seed of salvation. It also means that while your faith is sometimes fickle (like Jesus' disciples!), God's children can never lose their salvation.

Assurance of your status as God's child is cultivated through the responses and means outlined above; in particular, God's Word, prayer, and the sacraments. Although I did not mention it earlier, baptism is also an *assuring* mark of God's covenant-keeping promises: 'For the promise is for you and for your children' (Acts 2:39). God's Word, prayer, and the sacraments are the ordinary means by which God grows us, sanctifies us, and cultivates in us a greater assurance of his steadfast love.

I hope you have a better understanding of how we should respond amidst suffering. Thankfully, we are given tools and resources to help us along this journey. It is important to remember that you are not alone. God is with you as a refuge and strength and he calls you to cling to him as the greatest Treasure in the universe. Our response during seasons of suffering are directly related to our faith and assurance in God's character and promises.

5

FINDING HOPE

IN THE MIDST OF SUFFERING

As we have explored various aspects of suffering—from where suffering comes from to God's design for it in our lives, we also need to get very practical and put these pieces together. In this chapter, I want to present some very applicable counsel directly from Scripture for finding hope in the midst of suffering; a 'go-to guide' from the Bible to anchor your soul and hope to the eternal bedrock of God's abiding Word.

You may have the correct theology and you might have been preparing yourself for suffering, but now that it has come, you need handles of hope to grab onto. Let me simply share various portions of God's infinite wisdom and grace—that you may find and rest in a hopeful confidence in the God who cares.

TWENTY RELEVANT PASSAGES ON SUFFERING

Here are twenty of some of the most relevant and poignant Scripture passages that speak directly to a variety of afflictions—meant to give both a right perspective on your suffering as well as a God-dependent hope to endure.

Genesis 3:16-18

> To the woman [God] said, 'I will surely multiply your pain in childbearing; in pain you shall bring forth children. Your desire shall be for your husband, and he shall rule over you.' And to Adam he said, 'Because you have listened to the voice of your wife and have eaten of the tree of which I commanded you, 'You shall not eat of it,' cursed is the ground because of you; in pain you shall eat of it all the days of your life; thorns and thistles it shall bring forth for you; and you shall eat the plants of the field.

This is where suffering began. This is important to remember when you face trials of various kinds. Suffering should point us to our sin, and our sin should point us to the Savior who suffered on our behalf so that we would live without suffering with him forever. Knowing that suffering started with Adam's fall into sin helps put our present sufferings in their proper perspective.

Genesis 50:20

As for you, you meant evil against me, but God meant it for good.

Here, Joseph tells his brothers—who have sold him into slavery out of jealousy—that God overruled their evil intentions for his greater purpose. Maybe you feel abandoned and rejected by your own family or you are asking the question, 'Why me?' We do not know how our story will play out, but God does. In fact, 'We know that for those who love God all things work together for good, for those who are called according to his purpose' (Rom. 8:28).

Remember from chapter 2, God permits evil, restraints evil, and overrules evil for his good and sovereign purposes. This is illustrated here with the story of Joseph and his brothers.

Job 1:20-22

Then Job arose and tore his robe and shaved his head and fell on the ground and worshiped. And he said, 'Naked I came from my mother's womb, and naked shall I return. The LORD gave, and the LORD has taken away; blessed be the name of the LORD.' In all this Job did not sin or charge God with wrong.

By God's permission, Satan destroyed Job's property and killed his children. These verses are his response. It is hard to imagine the grief and pain caused by the death of one's children. Maybe you have been there yourself. But instead of lashing out in anger, run to God as the only true Source of comfort and hope. It is similar to the words found in Psalm 73:26, 'My flesh and my heart may fail, but God is the strength of my heart and my portion forever.' God is enough for us, and we oftentimes do not realize that truth until we have lost someone we love.

Psalm 23

> The LORD is my shepherd; I shall not want. He makes me lie down in green pastures. He leads me beside still waters. He restores my soul. He leads me in paths of righteousness for his name's sake. Even though I walk through the valley of the shadow of death, I will fear no evil, for you are with me; your rod and your staff, they comfort me. You prepare a table before me in the presence of my enemies; you anoint my head with oil; my cup overflows. Surely goodness and mercy shall follow me all the days of my life, and I shall dwell in the house of the LORD forever.

Few other passages in Scripture present such a comforting message of hope and security than Psalm 23. It carries us from the reality that our Shepherd-God provides for my every need. And when I am faced with danger and suffering, he is with me. The wonderful truth is that he will *always* be with us, on into his heavenly house forever. The Shepherd knows you and your needs. Jesus, the Good Shepherd, lays down his life for his sheep and he assures us: 'And no one will snatch them out of my hand' (John 10:28).

Psalm 46:1, 7, 10

God is our refuge and strength, a very present help in
trouble. The LORD of hosts is with us; the God of Jacob
is our fortress. Be still and know that I am God. I will be
exalted among the nations, I will be exalted in the earth!

This Psalm inspired Martin Luther to pen the Reformation hymn, 'A Mighty Fortress is Our God.' When
Luther faced the constant pressures of persecution by
Rome, he clung to God as a Source of strength and
security. Other Psalms communicate a similar theme.
King David wrote, 'The LORD is my rock and my fortress
and my deliverer, my God, my rock, in whom I take refuge,
my shield, and the horn of my salvation, my stronghold'
(Ps. 18:2; cf. Ps. 62:6-7). Note the terms used: *refuge,
fortress, rock, deliverer, stronghold*. They communicate

*Martin Luther (1483–1546) went to the city of Worms in 1521 to debate
with leading Roman Catholics about his writings, which they deemed
heretical. But instead of a debate, to his disappointment, they simply
requested that he 'recant.' But Luther could not renounce his faith in the
gospel or in the Scriptures. He said, 'Unless I am convinced by the testimony
of the Holy Scriptures or by evident reason-for I can believe neither pope
nor councils alone, as it is clear that they have erred repeatedly and
contradicted themselves-I consider myself convicted by the testimony of
Holy Scripture, which is my basis; my conscience is captive to the Word
of God. Thus I cannot and will not recant, because acting against one's
conscience is neither safe nor sound. God help me. Amen.' Upon leaving
Worms, Luther was captured by friends and taken to the Wartburg Castle,
where he undertook the work of translating the Bible into German. Here,
he battled the assaults of Satan and clung to God as his Mighty Fortress.*

strength and security. When you feel battered by the storms of affliction, you need to know that God remains unchanging, sure, and strong—like a mighty fortress! God is not shaken or troubled, but unwavering and rock-solid. Run to your Refuge and Strength!

Psalm 34:17-19

When the righteous cry for help, the LORD hears and delivers them out of all their troubles. The LORD is near to the brokenhearted and saves the crushed in spirit. Many are the afflictions of the righteous, but the LORD delivers him out of them all.

It is important to know that when you cry out to God, he hears your prayer. He is never so far away that he does not know your pain and hear your voice. In fact (as this Psalm records) God is especially 'near to the brokenhearted.' When Jesus was praying in the garden of Gethsemane before his arrest and subsequent crucifixion, he cried out that the cup of suffering might be removed from him. But—being obedient to death—Jesus submitted his human will to the divine will, 'Yet not what I will, but what you will' (Mark 14:36). We can have a similar trust in the God who knows us and hears our prayers in the midst of suffering and pain.

Psalm 42:3-6

My tears have been my food day and night, while they say to me all the day long, 'Where is your God?' These things I remember, as I pour out my soul: how I would go with the throng and lead them in procession to the house of God with glad shouts and songs of praise, a multitude keeping festival. Why are you cast down, O my soul, and why are you in turmoil within me? Hope in God; for I shall again praise him, my salvation and my God.

We see here an honest and raw pain. But notice that the Psalmist is talking *to* himself—'Why are you cast down, O my soul, and why are you in turmoil within me? Hope in God.' He is reminding himself of God's faithfulness and salvation. He is preaching, as it were, the gospel to himself! When you are dealing with illness, death, or pain, remind yourself of God's Word and God's character. Instead of listening to your heart, tell your heart the truth found in the Scriptures. If you run out of words to express, let God's Word be your mouthpiece. Simply read the Bible aloud and let his Word permeate and heal the wounds of your heart.

Psalm 119:49-50, 71

Remember your word to your servant, in which you have made me hope. This is my comfort in my affliction, that your promise gives me life. It is good for me that I was afflicted, that I might learn your statutes.

As you can see, the Psalms are replete with passages on the theme of suffering and pain, and how we can find hope in God. Here, affliction is seen as a sort of *school* where we 'learn' the Scriptures. In the academy of affliction, we learn God's design and purpose in suffering—that we might *experientially* believe the timeless truth of his Word.

After his affair with Bathsheba, King David cried out for God's forgiveness (recorded in Psalm 51). But he also petitions, 'Let the bones that you have broken rejoice' (v. 8) God brought him to a place of repentance through his internal grief and pain over what he had done. But, upon his repentance and forgiveness, he could look ahead to days of rejoicing. As the Apostle Paul wrote, 'I rejoice, not because you were grieved, but because you were grieved into repenting' (2 Cor. 7:9). Sometimes God breaks us so that he might heal us—molding us more and more into the image and likeness of Christ.

Lamentations 3:21-25

> But this I call to mind, and therefore I have hope: The steadfast love of the LORD never ceases; his mercies never come to an end; they are new every morning; great is your faithfulness. 'The LORD is my portion,' says my soul, 'therefore I will hope in him.' The LORD is good to those who wait for him, to the soul who seeks him.

Babylon destroyed Jerusalem in 587 BC and deported most of the Jews east to Babylon. Exiled to this foreign land—due to their sin—God's people suffered continual starvation and death. Lamentations describes this scene with vivid eyewitness descriptions. However, hope is the final word in this book and, here in chapter 3, we see this boldly pronounced.

What's remarkable about these verses is God's unchangeable and faithful mercy—'new every morning.' So we patiently endure and wait for him to teach us, mold us, and shape us more and more into the image of his Son, Jesus. God's mercies never come to an end; they will never run out. Why? Because 'the steadfast love of the LORD never ceases.' In the midst of suffering, despair, and pain, take time to intentionally seek the Lord and lay hold of him as your portion.

Habakkuk 3:17-18

> Though the fig tree should not blossom, nor fruit be on the vines, the produce of the olive fail and the fields yield no food, the flock be cut off from the fold and there be no herd in the stalls, yet I will rejoice in the LORD; I will take joy in the God of my salvation.

Habakkuk wondered why the wicked seemed to get away with injustice while God's people seemed to continually lack basic needs. He pleaded with God over these things. But, like Lamentations, it ends with a chorus of hope 'in the God of my salvation.' The various deprivations Habakkuk mentions are all essential to basic living: fruit trees, grapes, produce, olive oil, wheat, and animals all made up the basic ingredients of daily living.

Habakkuk is essentially saying that even though his basic physical needs should not be met—and thus suffer physical death and starvation—he would still be filled with joy and hope because he belongs to God. God could take *everything* from him and Habakkuk would still have enough. God is sufficient for you. If you have the true and living God as *your* God, you lack nothing.

John 9:1-3

As he passed by, he saw a man blind from birth. And his disciples asked him, 'Rabbi, who sinned, this man or his parents, that he was born blind?' Jesus answered, 'It was not that this man sinned, or his parents, but that the works of God might be displayed in him.

God ordains suffering so that he might receive the glory. Here, Jesus explains that the man's blindness did not come because of a particular sin. Sometimes, we begin to think in these categories: 'If I had only gone to church last Sunday, then I wouldn't have had that car wreck.' And sometimes our suffering is directly related to sin. However, we should see the positive side of suffering—*the works of God displayed*. How might God's works be displayed in your suffering? Where might you see the silver lining against the backdrop of pain?

Romans 5:3-5

Not only that, but we rejoice in our sufferings, knowing that suffering produces endurance, and endurance produces character, and character produces hope, and hope does not put us to shame, because God's love has been poured into our hearts through the Holy Spirit who has been given to us.

The apostle Paul outlines the positive progression, fruits, and effects of sufferings: *endurance*, *character*, and *hope*.

When we suffer, God creates greater endurance in us, which effectively changes our character. This character change from the inside out refocuses our ultimate hope on God and his love for us. As you have suffered—or are currently suffering—can you see this progression? The fact that you are reading this means that God might be right now producing greater character and hope!

Romans 8:18-22

> For I consider that the sufferings of this present time are not worth comparing with the glory that is to be revealed to us. For the creation waits with eager longing for the revealing of the sons of God. For the creation was subjected to futility, not willingly, but because of him who subjected it, in hope that the creation itself will be set free from its bondage to corruption and obtain the freedom of the glory of the children of God. For we know that the whole creation has been groaning together in the pains of childbirth until now.

Your suffering is one thread in a greater tapestry. The entire creation is subject to the effects and curse of the Fall (Gen. 3). With you, it waits with eager longing to be set free from its bondage to decay and corruption. With the birth, life, death, and resurrection of Jesus, that freedom has begun! The kingdom of God is continually *inbreaking* into this fallen world and will be brought to full completion at Christ's return. This means that our current sufferings 'are not worth comparing with the glory that is to be revealed.' While we might experience incredible pain in this life, it fails in comparison to the joy and freedom of sinlessness and corruption, when Jesus will make all things new.

Romans 8:35-39

Who shall separate us from the love of Christ? Shall tribulation, or distress, or persecution, or famine, or nakedness, or danger, or sword? As it is written, 'For your sake we are being killed all the day long; we are regarded as sheep to be slaughtered.' No, in all these things we are more than conquerors through him who loved us. For I am sure that neither death nor life, nor angels nor rulers, nor things present nor things to come, nor powers, nor height nor depth, nor anything else in all creation, will be able to separate us from the love of God in Christ Jesus our Lord.

It is easy to feel alone and abandoned, especially when suffering. You might feel that nobody understands and that you are worthless. Again from Romans 8, Paul reminds us that nothing—death, spiritual powers, or *anything* created—can pry God's love away from you. Because you are in Christ, God's full condemnation has been poured out on Jesus, there is now no condemnation for you. Thus, the sufferings you experience are not judgments of his wrath, but loving tokens of his discipline and sanctifying mercy. You are not alone or abandoned. Far from it; you are held by the never-letting-go love of God.

2 Corinthians 12:7-10

So to keep me from becoming conceited because of the surpassing greatness of the revelations, a thorn was given me in the flesh, a messenger of Satan to harass me, to keep me from becoming conceited. Three times I pleaded with the Lord about this, that it should leave me. But he said to me, 'My grace is sufficient for you, for my power is made perfect in weakness.' Therefore I will boast all the more gladly of my weaknesses, so that the power of Christ may rest upon me. For the sake of Christ, then, I am content with weaknesses, insults, hardships, persecutions, and calamities. For when I am weak, then I am strong.

You can imagine why Paul might have struggled with spiritual pride—under the inspiration of the Holy Spirit, he was writing Scripture! So to keep him humble, God (through Satan) gave him a 'thorn in the flesh.' We do not know exactly what his 'thorn' was, but it was nevertheless humbling. Even though he went through three different seasons pleading with God that it be removed, Jesus' answer was both firm and gentle: 'My grace is sufficient for you, for my power is made perfect in weakness.'

Paul's response was to *boast* in his weaknesses in order to magnify and exalt the power of Christ. He wanted Jesus to become greater in his life. Thus, he could be 'content' with whatever came his way—insults, persecutions, and sufferings. Sometimes, we experience sufferings so as to keep us humble and dependent upon the grace of God, which is sufficient for us. Therefore, we can find contentment in whatever lot we find ourselves.

Hebrews 11:32, 35–38

And what more shall I say? For time would fail me to tell of Gideon, Barak, Samson, Jephthah, of David and

Samuel and the prophets....Some were tortured, refusing to accept release, so that they might rise again to a better life. Others suffered mocking and flogging, and even chains and imprisonment. They were stoned, they were sawn in two, they were killed with the sword. They went about in skins of sheep and goats, destitute, afflicted, mistreated—of whom the world was not worthy—wandering about in deserts and mountains, and in dens and caves of the earth.

Many saints throughout history have suffered much worse than you or me. The author of Hebrews reminds us of the great heritage of those who have gone before us—the 'great cloud of witnesses' as he writes a few verses later. When I have suffered, God has reminded me of so many who have suffered far more and it puts my suffering in a bigger context and perspective. While I have experienced the death of close relatives and physical pain, I am not alone. This causes me to be thankful and grateful for all that God *has* provided!

James 1:2-4

Count it all joy, my brothers, when you meet trials of various kinds, for you know that the testing of your faith produces steadfastness. And let steadfastness have its full effect, that you may be perfect and complete, lacking in nothing.

Joy in suffering begins with a certain knowledge. What is that knowledge? It is the *testing* of your faith that produces a steadfast endurance so that you may grow up to complete spiritual maturity. James, therefore, echoes

Paul's statement in Romans 8 about suffering producing endurance and endurance, character. The various trials you meet are meant to test your faith—not because God does not know you or how you will respond—but so that you will know yourself, learn from the experience, and cling evermore to the promises of God.

1 Peter 2:21–23

For to this you have been called, because Christ also suffered for you, leaving you an example, so that you might follow in his steps. He committed no sin, neither was deceit found in his mouth. When he was reviled, he did not revile in return; when he suffered, he did not threaten, but continued entrusting himself to him who judges justly.

C. S. Lewis once remarked that only Jesus knew the full extent of temptation. When we are tempted, we will oftentimes give in. *But Jesus never gave in to temptation*, which means that he knew the full power and pull of its force. This is particularly true when we consider his unjust suffering and crucifixion. Suffering does not give us a justification and license to sin. Jesus not only suffered for us, but he suffered as an 'example' of how we ought to suffer. We are not to respond with like sin, but rather entrust ourselves to our faithful and just Father.

1 Peter 4:12–16

Beloved, do not be surprised at the fiery trial when it comes upon you to test you, as though something strange were happening to you. But rejoice insofar as you share Christ's sufferings, that you may also rejoice and be glad when his glory is revealed. If you are insulted for the name of Christ, you are blessed, because the Spirit of glory and of God rests upon you. But let none of you suffer as a murderer or a thief or an evildoer or as a meddler. Yet if anyone suffers as a Christian, let him not be ashamed, but let him glorify God in that name.

Similar to James' instruction on trials being a 'test,' Peter also affirms this truth—it is meant to *test* you as a purifying fire removing the dross. But we should not be surprised by suffering; rather, we are to expect it. In particular, we should expect the suffering that comes as persecution to our faith. We should expect the world to hate us because it hated the One to whom we belong, Jesus (cf. John 15:18-19). As Paul wrote, 'all who desire to live a godly life in Christ Jesus will be persecuted' (2 Tim. 3:12). Suffering is par for the course, the norm. We should, therefore, expect it and prepare for it.

Revelation 21:3-5

And I heard a loud voice from the throne saying, 'Behold, the dwelling place of God is with man. He will dwell with them, and they will be his people, and God himself will be with them as their God. He will wipe away every tear from their eyes, and death shall be no more, neither shall there be mourning, nor crying, nor pain anymore, for the former things have passed away.' And he who was seated on the throne said, 'Behold, I am making all things new.'

There is no greater assurance and promise than this truth: God is our God and we are his people. This is the substance of God's covenant throughout history. From beginning to end, God is unfolding his amazing story of redemption and will bring his people to a place where there is no more pain, suffering, or mourning. In fact, he will make 'all things new.' When we cross that great river of death, we shall hear, 'When you pass through the waters, I will be with you; and through the rivers, they shall not overwhelm you…for I am the LORD your God' (Isa. 43:2-3).

FURTHER SCRIPTURE READING ON SUFFERING

Psalm 30:4-12; 55:22
Isaiah 41; 43:1-7
John 16:20-33
1 Corinthians 15:50-58
2 Corinthians 4:8-18
Philippians 4:11-13
Colossians 1:24
1 Thessalonians 3:3
2 Timothy 1:8-12
James 5:10

6

MINISTERING TO SUFFERERS

You might have picked up this brief guide to suffering because someone you know and love is facing a very challenging season of suffering. It is important to realize that, although you have been equipped with biblical truth as it relates to pain and affliction, you need to share this biblical truth with great care, sensitivity, gentleness, and love. Indeed, we should demonstrate these characteristics when communicating *any* truth!

Sometimes, I feel so confident in having the right theology on suffering that I almost forget about the sufferer. It can be similar to the task of apologetics (defending the faith). We can easily get so caught up in winning the argument, that we neglect concern over the salvation of the person with whom we are debating. This is why Peter cautions that we are always to be prepared to make a defense of the faith, but to 'do it with gentleness and respect' (1 Pet. 3:16). Paul urges his Ephesian readers: 'Speaking the truth in love, we are to grow up in every way' (Eph. 4:15). So truth and love, *together*, form the twin tools of ministering to sufferers.

But we cannot cover up the truth with empty clichés either. It might be easier and politically correct to simply say, 'My thoughts and prayers are with you' and leave it at that. Or, it might be easy to not say *anything* about the truth, which really is the most *un*loving thing you can do! Yes, sometimes, you need not say anything, but simply be with someone grieving. And that is fine, for a short time. But if they never receive truth, it will be a long and difficult road for him or her.

I have seen truth and love neglected so many times in my own attempts to minister to sufferers, that I am sure others have experienced this polarization as well. Thus, while it is very important to have a good biblical theology of suffering—as we have outlined in this book—it is *also* very important to communicate sensitivity and tenderness along with the truth. We cannot avoid either truth or love; they *together* bring healing and hope.

Do you have a natural proclivity toward either truth or love in how you speak with people? Do you have a difficult time saying what really needs to be said out of a sense of love? Or do you have a difficult time showing love in your desire to communicate the truth?

SIX WAYS TO MINISTER TO SUFFERERS

As you *prepare* yourself to suffer, here are six practical ways to minister to others who are suffering, based on some of the points made throughout this book:

Realize that Suffering (in and of itself) Is not Evil

Although the two are often coupled together, suffering is the *effect* and *consequence* of sin—stemming from Eden—but ultimately used by God to display his glory, for the good of his people, and the judgment of those who continue to reject him. This simple distinction can go a long way in your thinking and ministry with the sufferer.

The suffering might have come at the hands of an evil act, but the suffering itself is not evil and even has a greater purpose in the eyes of God. He overrules the evil act for his glory and your ultimate good. Realizing this distinction can change the perspective on the situation and provide a door to seeing the possibilities of how God is using this in the sufferer's life. As you consider the reasons outlined in the pages above, how might this important distinction help separate the evil intention and act of another and God's use of the suffering in the person's life?

Similarly, we should not presume upon God's intentions with suffering. Simply because a tornado ripped through a town does not necessarily mean that God is judging that town for some specific sin they did. That would be presuming upon God's greater purposes and design; to possess his wisdom and knowledge. Therefore, we should be like Job's three 'friends,' who tried to make direct correlation between Job's suffering and his sin. While it is certainly true that our sin often brings about pain, presuming upon God's intentions is *not* how we should minister to sufferers.

Don't Apologize for God

We mustn't respond to someone's suffering like many celebrity 'evangelical' leaders who respond to tragedy. They will oftentimes say, 'Surely, God didn't allow this' or 'God couldn't help what happened.' Sometimes, self-professing Christians seem embarrassed by God's attributes, especially his sovereignty. But God is both sovereign *and* good. While sufferers probably do not need a lesson on the intricacies of God's decrees, we should not run to the opposite pole to apologize for him or why he has brought to us rods of affliction. Sufferers need a true Refuge and Strength in times of trouble, not a weak and impotent bellhop.

Similarly, God is at the front and center of every aspect of our lives, from beginning to end. He does not 'disappear' when we face trials. For some, it is easy simply to not even talk about God or his purposes when we experience suffering. When we suffer, we should seek and strive for greater fellowship with the true and living God as he is revealed in Scripture. Only the *true* God can offer true hope and healing. Other 'gods' are empty idols. Therefore, we should not shrink from declaring the full array of God's character to help someone during seasons of suffering.

We should not be ashamed of God or of the Scriptures. Sometimes, I think we can have a functional embarrassment of certain 'difficult' portions of Scripture, but we do not need to be embarrassed. It is God's Word, not ours. We are called to faithfully present its truth rather than trying to be the arbiters of truth.

Listen with Love, First

Even though you might be prepared to give the ten theological reasons for human suffering, sufferers need to know that you care. Actively listen—with physical expression, supporting questions, and appropriate responses. For you to accurately understand the sufferer's heart-issues and the true source of his or her pain, it takes intentional listening. Sometimes, listening is enough. Words can (and should) come later, but listening is sometimes enough.

The art of listening might actually take some practice, as many of us tend to talk a lot about ourselves and interrupt others. Interestingly, when you go into a situation with the intent of listening, you end up asking better, more probing questions because you are truly trying to *hear* them and their struggles.

When I do pastoral visits to hospitals and nursing homes, I try to have this attitude going in. I am here to offers words of truth and hope—which I will typically read from Scripture—but I am also here to *listen*. Sometimes I get nervous because I am afraid I will not have the right words to say. But if I am intent on listening, this is never an issue. Visitations become rather simple with this approach.

Point Them and Lead Them to the Means of Grace

God's Word, prayer, and the sacraments—enjoyed in a worshipful community of faith—provide the ordinary means whereby God both saves and sanctifies his children under trial. Please read that again. These are the apostolic, God-ordained means of planting and watering the gospel seed in the dry ground of a broken soul.

Children of God, especially *suffering* children of God, need to be nourished and filled with God's Word, prayer, and Communion at the Lord's Table. Nothing can replace these most basic means of growing through affliction. When we suffer, we will sometimes sinfully neglect all three, thinking that will help. It does not. But rather than simply telling a sufferer that they need the means of grace, lead them to the means of grace by loving them yourself. In other words, inspire them to long for God's Word by longing for it yourself. Encourage them in a season of prayer by leading them in prayer. Nothing motivates and inspires people to avail themselves to the means of grace like your own love and passion for them.

Follow Through with Community

Ministry to a sufferer should not be a one-time event. I have seen the tragedy of this over and over again. For example, somebody in your church has gone through surgery or a painful season. They need some help and meals and so the church rallies around them with plenty of food—*for two weeks at most*. Then, they are forgotten. Nobody follows up, nobody continues to actively care, and nobody continues the meals. It is important to follow up regularly and be willing to bear his or her burdens as long as needed—striving to equip the saints for the work of ministry as a community around the sufferer.

Some sufferers tend to draw away from people, community, and even their own daily life altogether. They isolate themselves and it has the effect of driving them deeper and deeper into despair. While it is perfectly acceptable to give sufferers space, their souls need regular nourishment from God's Word, prayer, and the sacraments experienced within the community of faith. They need this community to come alongside them and around them so that they can hear God's words of promise: 'Cast your burden on the LORD, and he will sustain you' (Ps. 55:22).

The apostle Paul wrote to the Corinthians, 'God of all comfort, who comforts us in all our affliction, so that we may be able to comfort those who are in any affliction, with the comfort with which we ourselves are comforted by God' (2 Cor. 1:3-4). In the community of faith, we extend comfort to sufferers as we have experienced comfort from God. While they receive direct comfort from the Lord, they also receive comfort from the body—the hands and feet—of Christ.

Apply the Balm of the Gospel

We have a High Priest who sympathizes with our weakness and suffering, for he was the greatest Sufferer. Because of his life, death, and resurrection, all things work for good for those who love God and are called according to his purpose. As adopted children of God, encourage sufferers to cling to the promises of the gospel that God, by his never-letting-go love is weaning them from this world for the world to come.

We never move past our need for the gospel. It is always informing, always supporting, always pointing us to the grace of God in our lives. It reminds us that the true source of our salvation and status as God's people comes not from ourselves or our 'good works,' but from God who has shown us mercy. The *good news* is just as relevant in the midst of suffering as it is on the first day you believed. Reminding sufferers of this good news— what God has done in Christ in his life, death, and resurrection for sinners—is the best words you can offer. It helps a sufferer regain perspective, rest in the security of eternal hope, and even find a sense of inner joy and peace under trial.

As we face trials of various kinds, may we not be tempted by the fading fads of our culture or the empty clichés of shallow 'Christianese,' but rather immerse ourselves with the eternal truth of the Scriptures, letting them transform us by the renewing of our minds, that we may discern what is the will of God—what is good and acceptable and perfect, even during seasons of suffering.

May God fill our souls with an unshakable delight in him—the strength of our hearts and portion forever.

While noting and even emulating historic or contemporary examples of saints who have suffered well, we should not forget that we have already been given the greatest hope in the midst of suffering: the gospel of Jesus Christ. In season and out of season, Jesus' work in his life, death, and resurrection for you is truly good news. Remembering this helps put present afflictions in their proper perspective.

SUGGESTIONS FOR FURTHER READING

Alcorn, Randy. *If God is Good: Faith in the Midst of Suffering and Evil.* Colorado Springs: Multnomah Books, 2009.

Bridges, Jerry. *Trusting God: Even When Life Hurts.* Colorado Springs: NavPress, 2008.

Carson, D. A. *How Long, O Lord? Reflections on Suffering and Evil.* Grand Rapids: Baker Academic, 2006.

Cosby, Brian H. *Suffering and Sovereignty: John Flavel and the Puritans on Afflictive Providence.* Grand Rapids: Reformation Heritage Books, 2012.

Duncan, Ligon. *Does Grace Grow Best in Winter?* Phillipsburg, NJ: P&R Publishing, 2009.

Flavel, John. *The Mystery of Providence* (Puritan Paperbacks). Edinburgh: The Banner of Truth Trust, 1963.

Guthrie, Nancy, Ed. *Be Still, My Soul: Embracing God's Purpose and Provision in Suffering.* Wheaton: Crossway Books, 2010.

Keller, Timothy. *Walking with God through Pain and Suffering.* New York: Dutton, 2013.

McCartney, Dan. *Why Does it Have to Hurt? The Meaning of Christian Suffering.* Phillipsburg, NJ: P&R Publishing, 1998.

Morgan, Christopher W. and Robert A. Peterson, Eds. *Suffering and the Goodness of God.* Wheaton: Crossway Books, 2008.

Piper, John and Justin Taylor, Eds. *Suffering and the Sovereignty of God.* Wheaton: Crossway Books, 2006.

Sibbes, Richard. *The Bruised Reed* (Puritan Paperbacks). Edinburgh: The Banner of Truth Trust, 1998.

Tada, Joni Eareckson. *When God Weeps: Why Our Sufferings Matter to the Almighty.* Grand Rapids: Zondervan, 1997.

ENDNOTES

1 Bertrand Russell, 'A Free Man's Worship' in *Modern Essays*, selected by Christopher Morley (New York: Harcourt, Brace and Company, 1921), 265.

2 Richard Dawkins, *River Out of Eden: A Darwinian View of Life* (London: Basic Books, 1996), 132-33.

3 Quoted in Micah Sandusky, Jeremiah Keenan, Hannah Victor, and Faith Concepcion, *The Daily Pennsylvanian* (February 9, 2014). Accessed at thedp.com.

4 John Piper, *When the Darkness Will Not Lift: Doing What We Can While We Wait for God—and Joy* (Wheaton: Crossway Books, 2006), 61-62.

5 John Flavel, *A Token for Mourners* in *The Works of John Flavel*, 6 Volumes (Edinburgh: The Banner of Truth Trust, 1968), 5:626. Similarly, he writes, 'Suffering is but a *respective*, *external*, and *temporal* evil; but sin in an universal, internal, and everlasting evil' (*Preparation for Sufferings*, 6:63).

6 Omnipresence means that the creator God is everywhere present (Job 34:21; Ps. 139:7-10; Prov. 15:3; Jer. 23:24; Matt. 18:20).

7 For a good description of this, see John Flavel, *An Exposition of the (Westminster) Assembly's Shorter Catechism*, 6:165.

8 Thomas Watson, *The Art of Divine Contentment* (London: Printed by T. M. for Ralph Smith, at the sign of the Bible at Cornhil, near the Royal Exchange, 1654), 3.

9 Francis Bremer and Tom Webster, eds. *Puritans and Puritanism in Europe and America: A Comprehensive Encyclopedia* (Santa Barbara, CA: ABC-CLIO, 2006), 45.

10 Westminster Shorter Catechism, Q. 11.

11 For a more extensive survey of these, see Brian H. Cosby, *Suffering and Sovereignty: John Flavel and the Puritans on Afflictive Providence* (Grand Rapids: Reformation Heritage Books, 2012).

12 Westminster Shorter Catechism, Q. 35.

13 Flavel, *The Balm of the Covenant*, 6:105.

14 Flavel, *Preparations for Sufferings*, 6:18.

15 For a number of these, see Chapter 5.

16 Thomas Watson, *A Body of Practical Divinity, in a Series of Sermons on the Westminster Shorter Catechism* (Aberdeen: George King, 1838), 230.

Other books in the Series

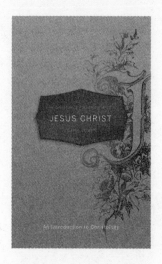

A Christian's Pocket Guide to Jesus Christ
An Introduction to Christology
MARK JONES
ISBN 978-1-84550-951-4

A Christian's Pocket Guide to Baptism
The Water that Divides
ROBERT LETHAM
ISBN 978-1-84550-968-2

A Christian's Pocket Guide to Being Made Right With God
Understanding Justification
GUY WATERS
ISBN 978-1-78191-109-9

A Christian's Pocket Guide to Growing in Holiness
Understanding Sanctification
J. V. FESKO
ISBN 978-1-84550-810-4

Christian Focus Publications

Our mission statement –

STAYING FAITHFUL
In dependence upon God we seek to impact the world
through literature faithful to His infallible Word, the
Bible. Our aim is to ensure that the Lord Jesus Christ is
presented as the only hope to obtain forgiveness of sin, live
a useful life and look forward to heaven with Him.

Our books are published in four imprints:

CHRISTIAN
FOCUS

Popular works including biographies, commentaries, basic
doctrine and Christian living.

CHRISTIAN
HERITAGE

Books representing some of
the best material from the
rich heritage of the church.

MENTOR

Books written at a level suit-
able for Bible College and
seminary students, pastors,
and other serious readers.
The imprint includes com-
mentaries, doctrinal studies,
examination of current issues
and church history.

CF4•K

Children's books for quality
Bible teaching and for all age
groups: Sunday school curricu-
lum, puzzle and activity books;
personal and family devotional
titles, biographies and inspira-
tional stories – Because you are
never too young to know Jesus!

Christian Focus Publications Ltd,
Geanies House, Fearn, Ross-shire,
IV20 1TW, Scotland, United Kingdom.
www.christianfocus.com